IT HAD TO BE TOLD! ™
PUBLISHING

I want to tell you a story...
ONE THAT I STILL CAN'T BELIEVE! ™

Copyright © 2017 by It Had To Be Told Publishing, LLC.

"I want to tell you a story, one that I still can't believe"
and "It Had To Be Told" are trademarks of
It Had To Be Told Publishing, LLC.
All other trademarks belong to their respective owners.

All rights reserved. This book or any portion thereof may not be
reproduced or used in any manner whatsoever without the
express written permission of the publisher except for the use
of brief quotations in a book review.

ISBN -- 978-0-9989440-2-9

It Had To Be Told Publishing,
Tampa, Florida
www.ItHadToBeTold.com

This book has been proudly produced and printed
in the United States of America

By Jeff Attinella
Illustrated by David Capalungan

I want to tell you a story, one that I still can't believe.
The story of a race long ago,
the biggest the world had ever seen!

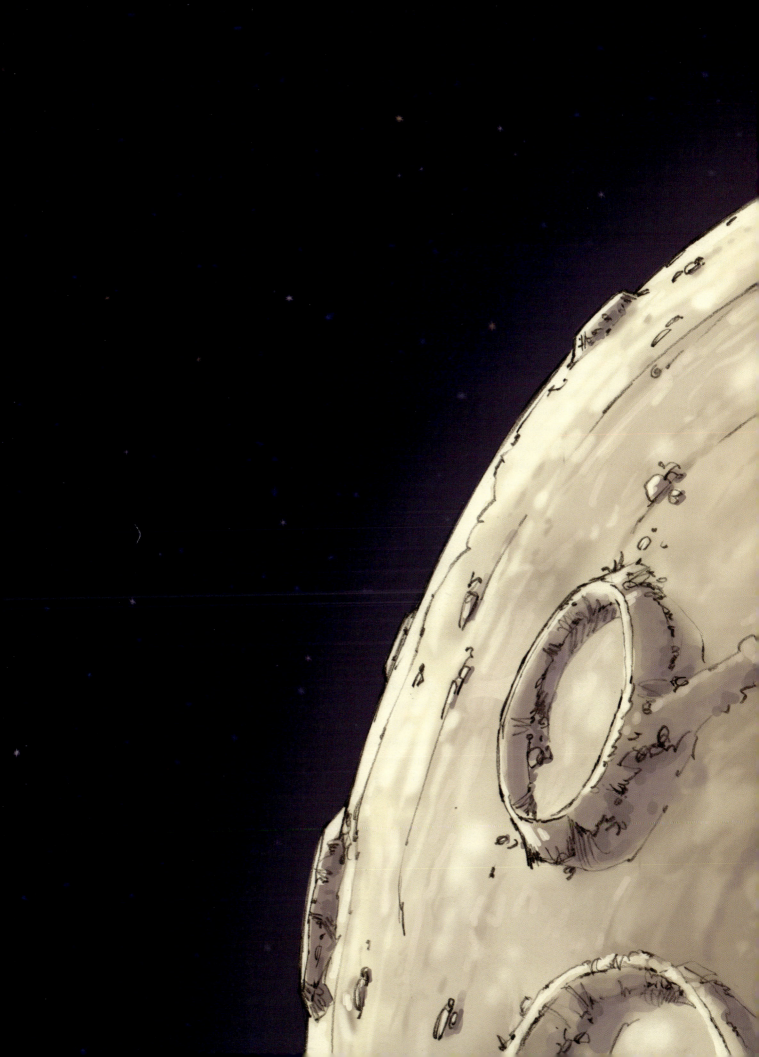

It was the race to the moon and it's really a true story,
a race between two countries competing for world-wide glory.

Russia and the United States were out to prove who was best; putting a man on the moon would be the ultimate test.

In 1955, the "Space Race" was all the talk.
Two world powers stepped up to the starting block.

In 1957, Russia launched Sputnik One and jumped to an early lead.

With the unmanned satellite in orbit,
Russia was quickly gaining speed.

One year later, America launched Explorer 1 to claim their spot in space.
With a satellite of its own in orbit, the U.S. matched Russia's pace.

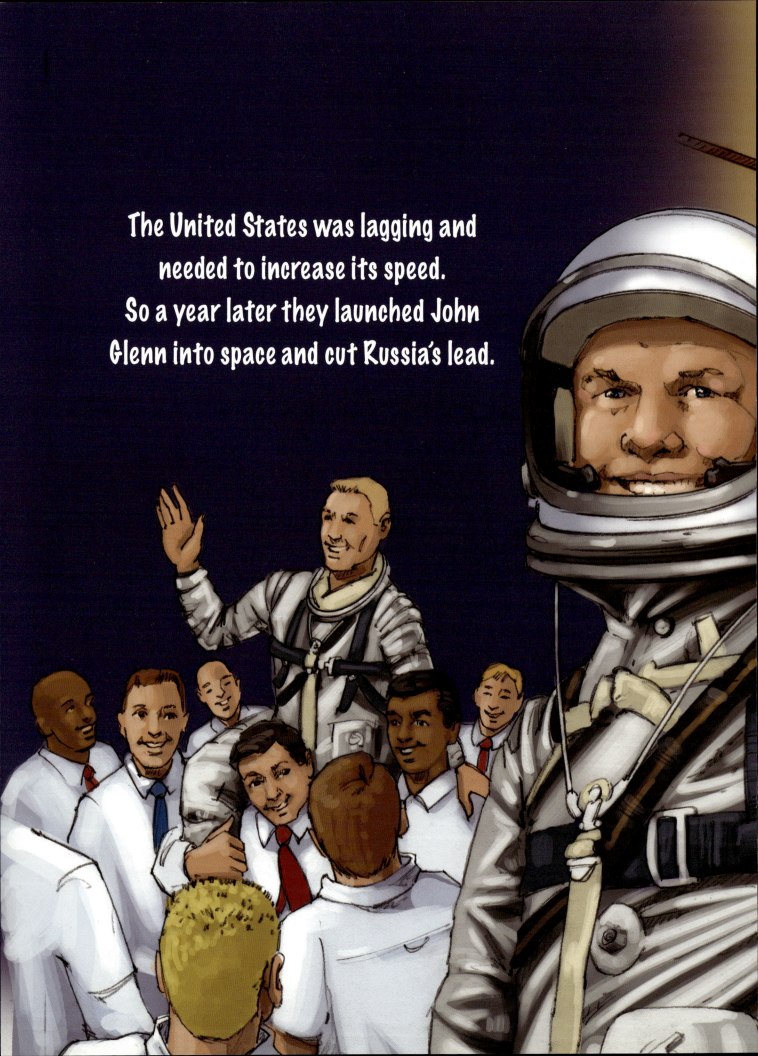

Russia was moving fast, but America was right on its tail. President John F. Kennedy wanted to ensure the U.S. would prevail.

In a 1962 speech to the country, JFK shared a dream that was bold. He wanted to win the Space Race, but that's not all, the people were told.

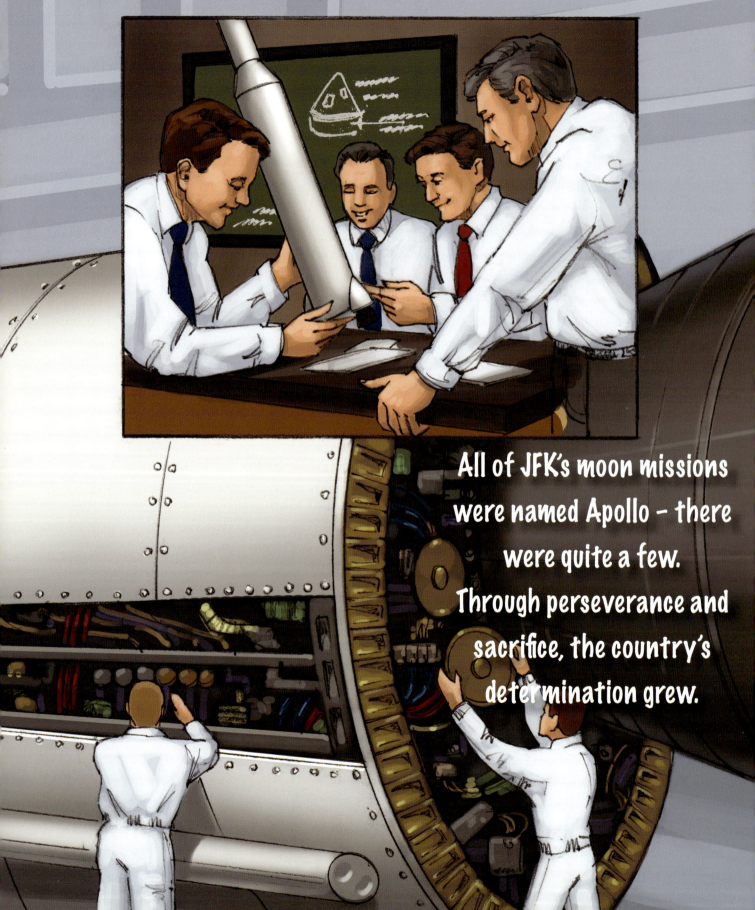

Apollo 1 was the first scheduled space flight, but something went very wrong. The spacecraft never made it to the launch pad so the mission didn't last long.

The U.S. team got back to work but the next mission would wait. It was important to get things just right, to avoid Apollo 1's fate.

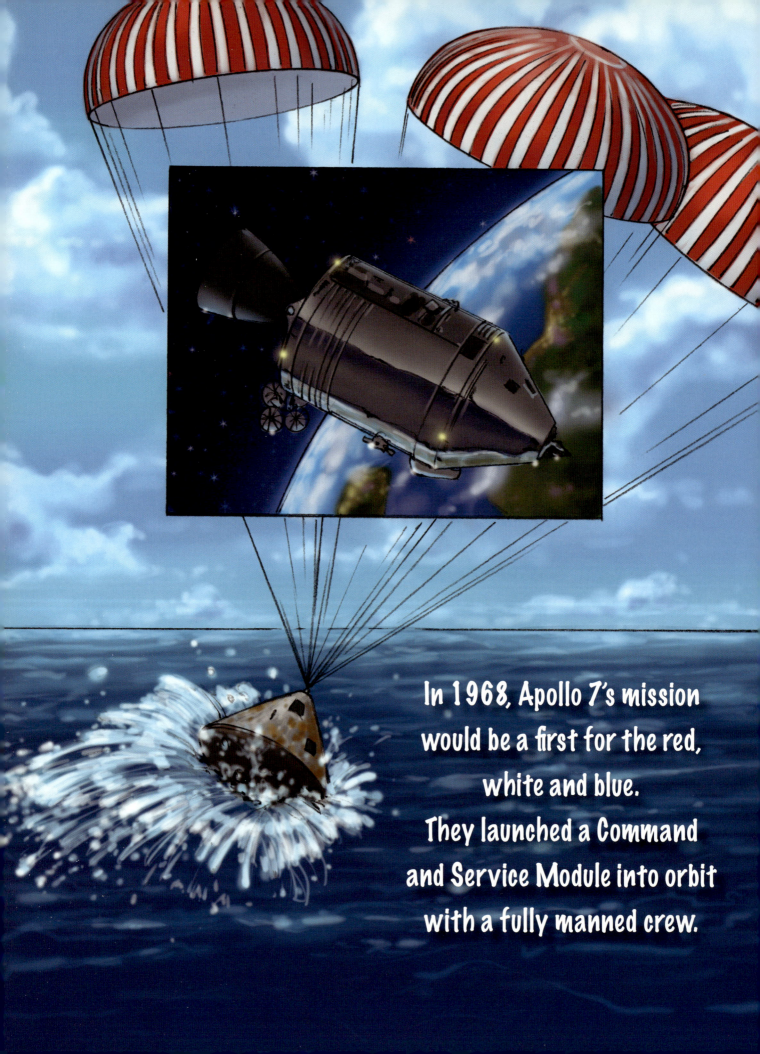

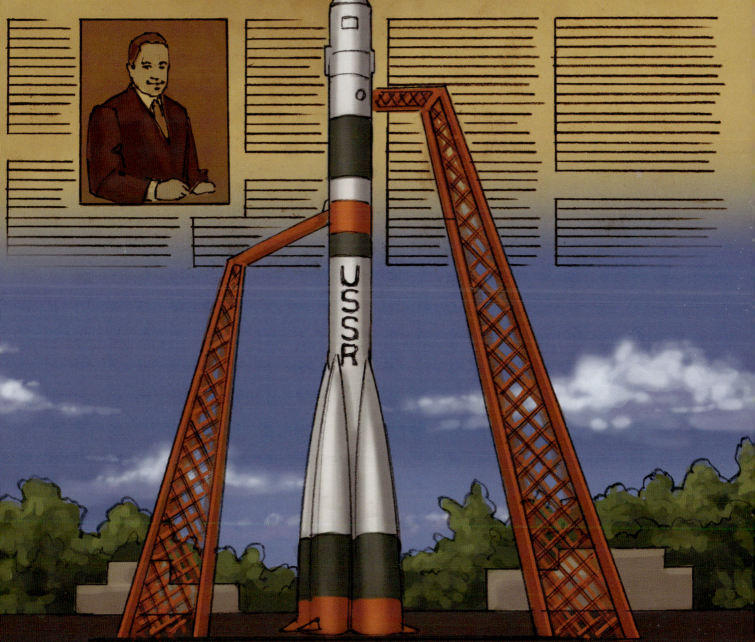

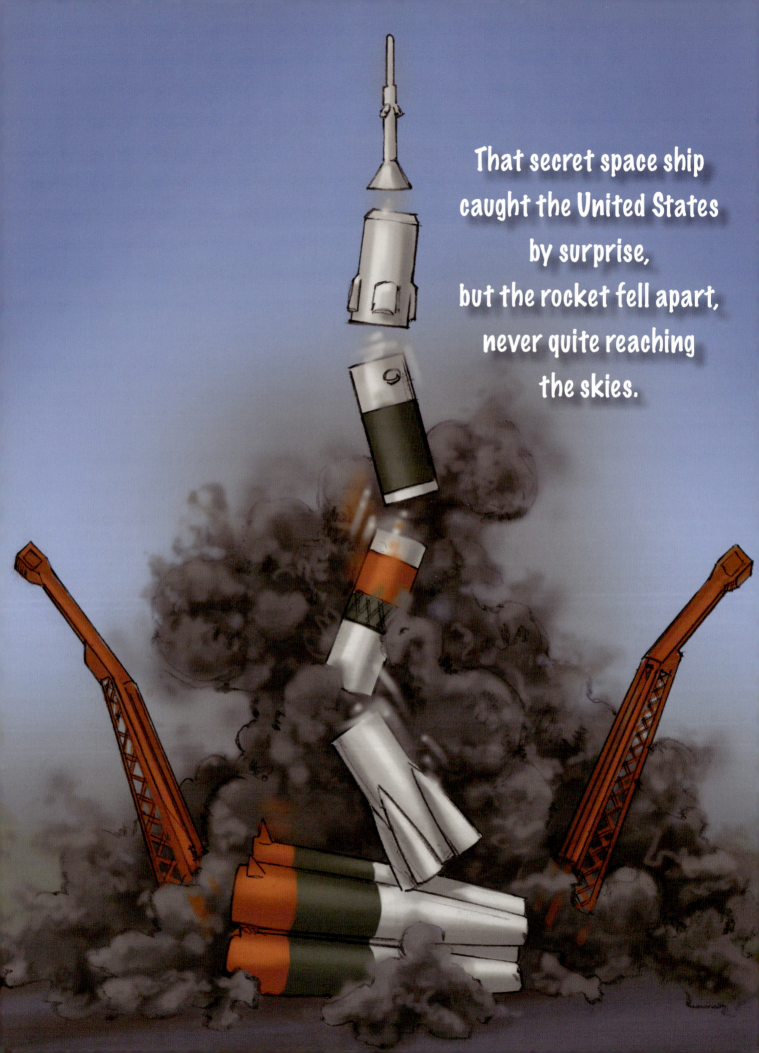

That cleared the way for the U.S. to win once and for all.
...and on July 16, 1969, Apollo 11 answered the call.

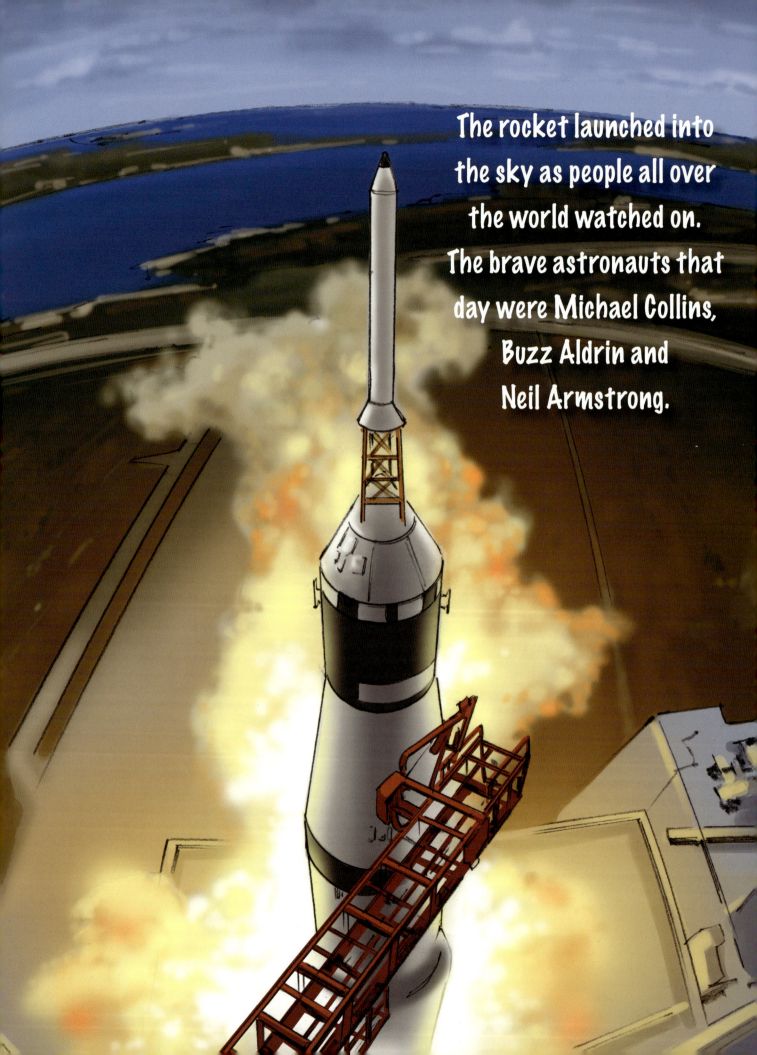

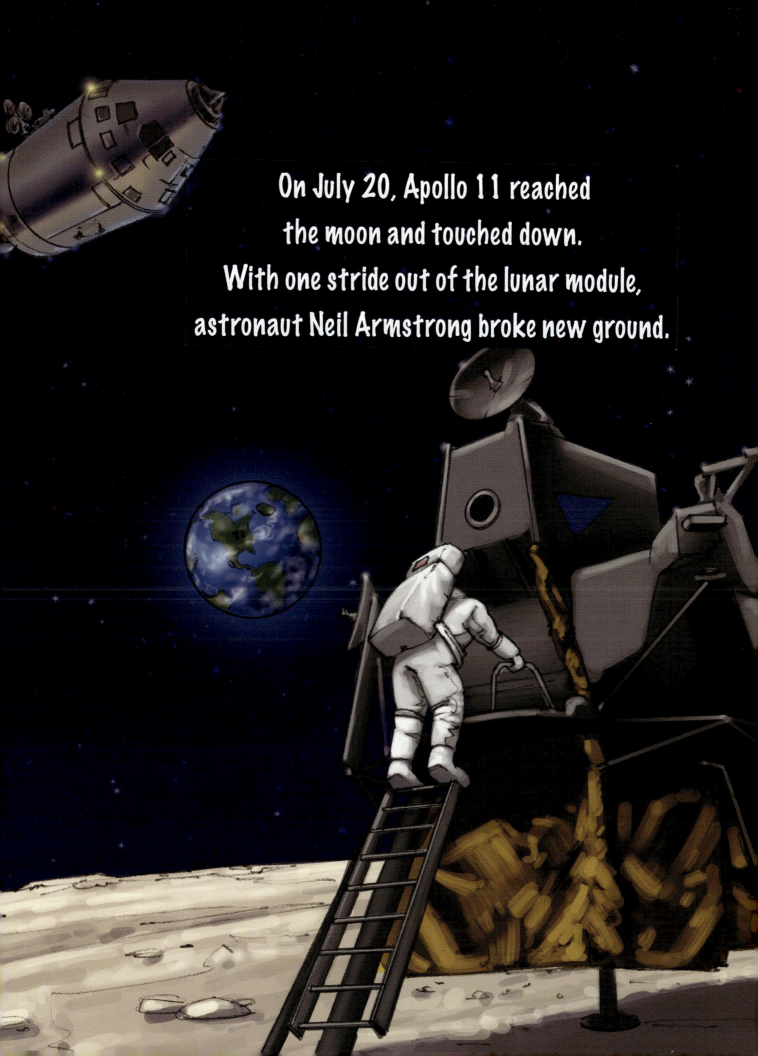

On July 20, Apollo 11 reached the moon and touched down. With one stride out of the lunar module, astronaut Neil Armstrong broke new ground.

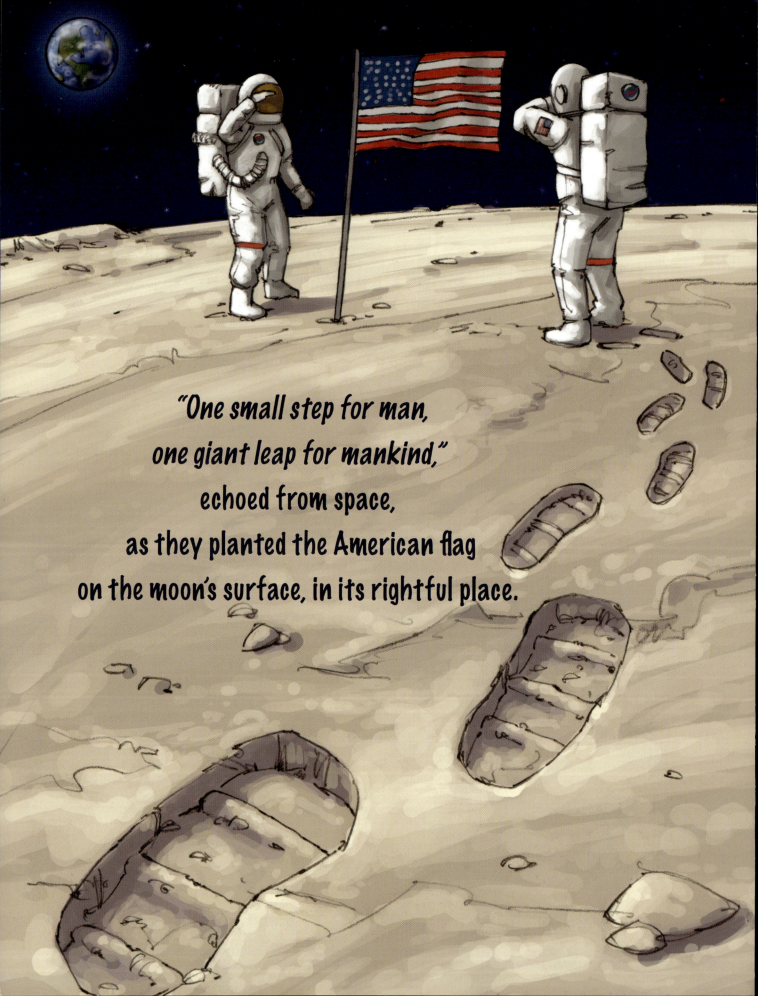

In a time of racing with the Russians to see who was number one, it was the United States making history and having all the fun.

As for the Russians, it wasn't considered a total loss, but as for putting a man on the moon? Well, that dream was tossed!

When the Space Race came to an end, peace became the new theme, and as the years went on, the two countries worked as a team.

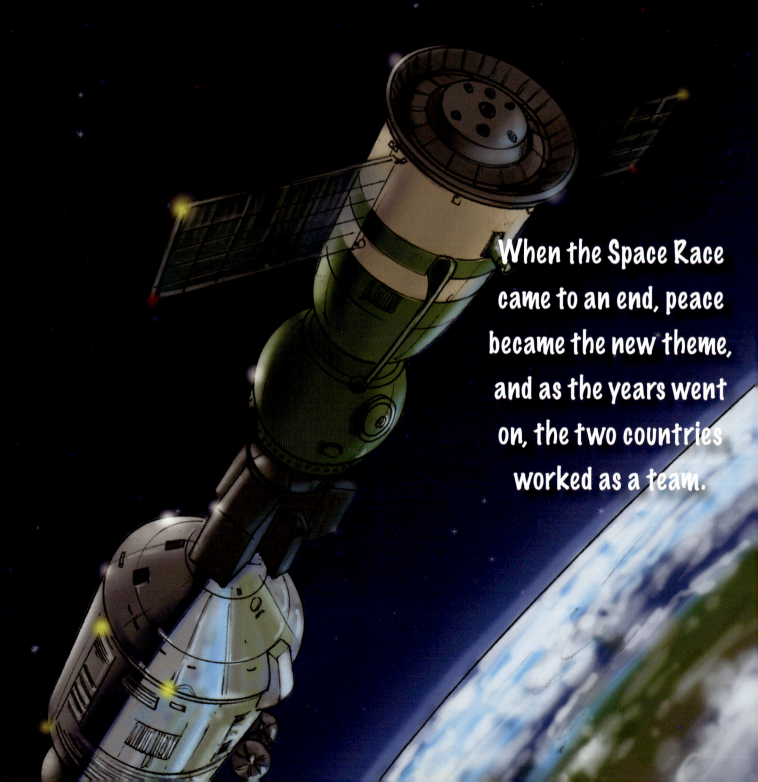

In 1975, the U.S. and Russia conducted a joint mission in space, eir ships docked together and the crews exchanged gifts face to face.

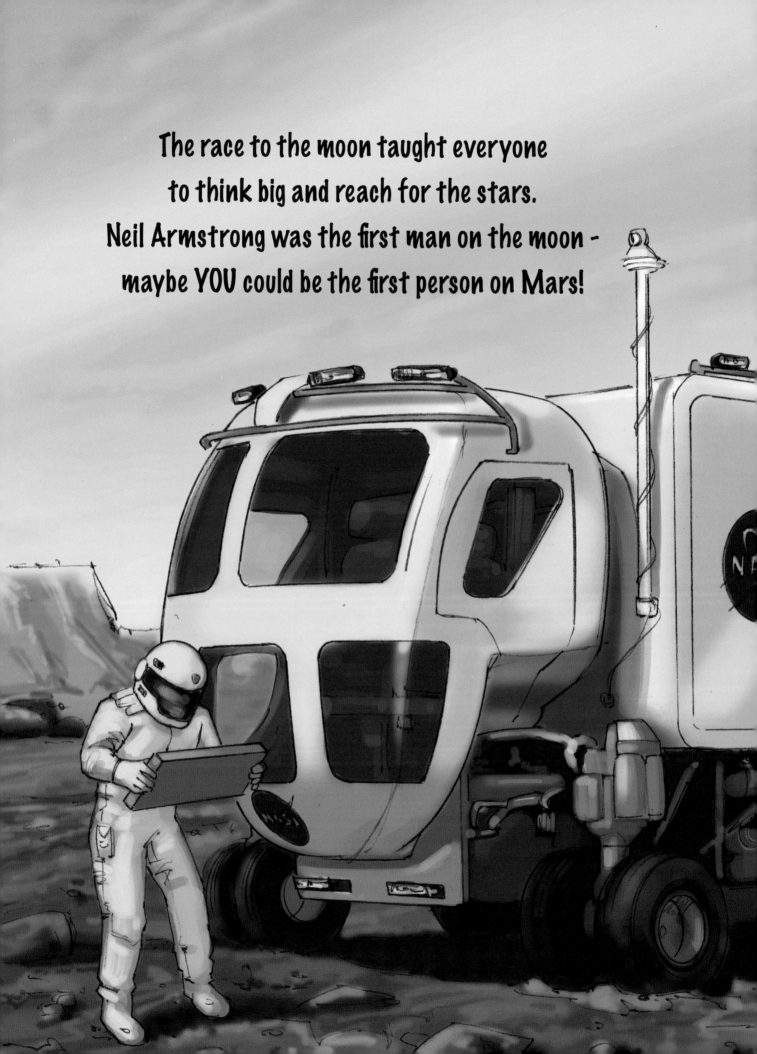

The race to the moon taught everyone to think big and reach for the stars. Neil Armstrong was the first man on the moon - maybe YOU could be the first person on Mars!

DID YOU KNOW?

1. TODAY'S RUSSIA WAS CALLED THE SOVIET UNION DURING THE "SPACE RACE." THE SOVIET UNION OR THE UNION OF SOVIET SOCIALIST REPUBLICS (USSR) WAS FOUNDED IN 1922 AND WAS DISSOLVED IN 1991.

2. NEIL ARMSTRONG EARNED HIS PILOT'S LICENSE BEFORE HE WAS ABLE TO LEGALLY DRIVE.

3. THE SATURN V ROCKET USED FOR THE APOLLO 11 MISSION WAS 363 FEET HIGH, 58 FEET TALLER THAN THE STATUE OF LIBERTY.

4. A TOTAL OF 841.6 POUNDS OF LUNAR ROCKS WERE BROUGHT BACK FROM SIX APOLLO FLIGHTS. THE APOLLO PROGRAM COST 24 BILLION DOLLARS. THAT'S APPROXIMATELY $28,500 PER POUND!

5. THE APOLLO COMPUTER HAD LESS COMPUTING POWER THAN AN EARLY CELL PHONE.

6. THE MOON IS, ON AVERAGE, 239,000 MILES FROM EARTH.

7. NEIL ARMSTRONG AND BUZZ ALDRIN HAD TO REMEMBER TO LEAVE THE DOOR TO THE LUNAR MODULE LANDER SLIGHTLY AJAR BECAUSE IT HAD NO OUTSIDE DOOR HANDLE.

8. THE WALLS OF THE LUNAR MODULE'S ASTRONAUT COMPARTMENT WERE THINNER THAN THREE LAYERS OF ALUMINUM FOIL.

9. NEIL ARMSTRONG AND BUZZ ALDRIN LEFT ONE OF RUSSIAN COSMONAUT, YURI GAGARIN'S MEDALS ON THE MOON TO PAY TRIBUTE TO HIS ACCOMPLISHMENT AS THE FIRST MAN IN SPACE.

10. THE UNMANNED SOVIET PROBE, LUNA 15, CRASHED INTO THE MOON'S SURFACE WHILE NEIL ARMSTRONG AND BUZZ ALDRIN WERE STILL ON IT. THE TWO SPACE CRAFTS WERE A LITTLE OVER 740 MILES APART.

11. BUZZ ALDRIN CLAIMED TRAVEL EXPENSES FOR HIS TRIP TO THE MOON, TOTALLING $33.31.

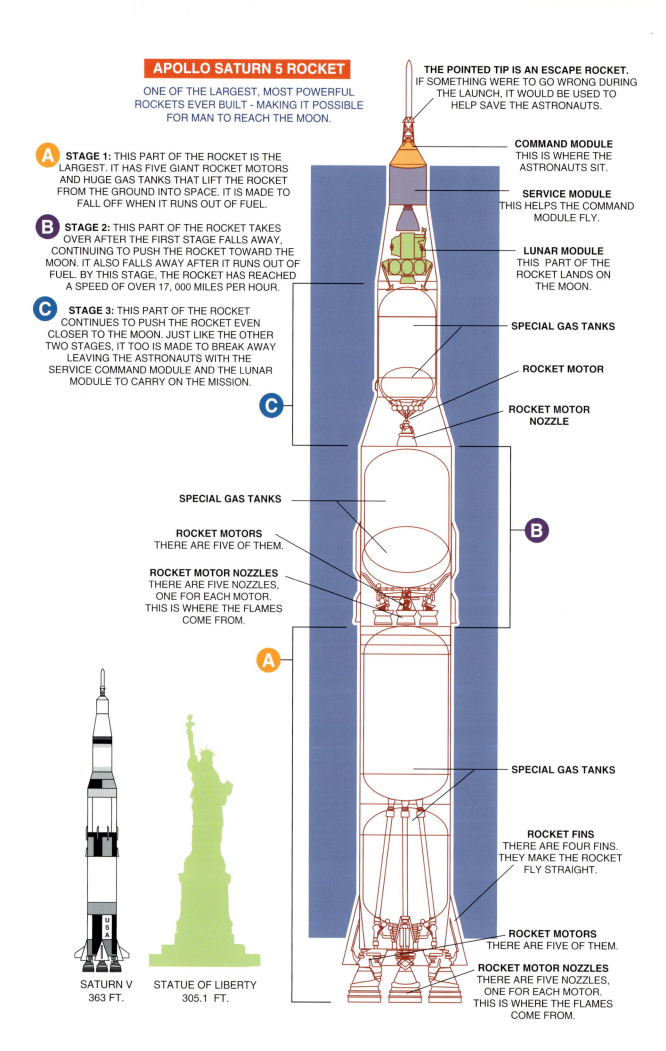

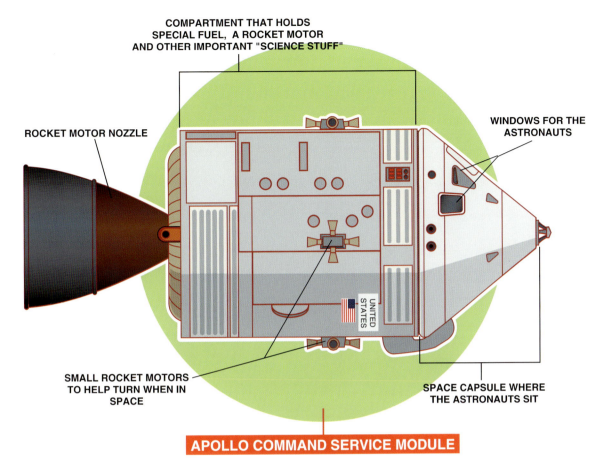

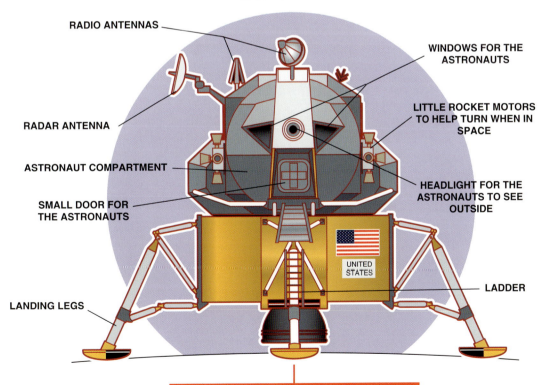

TECHNICAL ILLUSTRATIONS BY SCOTT FLEENOR

IT HAD TO BE TOLD!™ PUBLISHING

I want to tell you a story...
ONE THAT I STILL CAN'T BELIEVE!™

It is our mission to promote children's literacy nationwide. Through our books, we hope to inspire a lifelong love of reading by touching the hearts of children and adults alike.